ANGLO-S_____
ENGLAND
400–790

Sally Crawford

SHIRE LIVING HISTORIES

How we worked • How we played • How we lived

Published in Great Britain in 2011 by Shire Publications Ltd, Midland House, West Way, Botley, Oxford OX2 0PH, United Kingdom.

44-02 23rd Street, Suite 219, Long Island City, NY 11101, USA.

E-mail: shire@shirebooks.co.uk   www.shirebooks.co.uk

A CIP catalogue record for this book is available from the British Library.

Shire Living Histories no. 11.   ISBN-13: 978 0 74780 836 7

Sally Crawford has asserted her right under the Copyright, Designs and Patents Act, 1988, to be identified as the author of this book.

Designed by Myriam Bell Design, France and typeset in Perpetua, Janson Text and Gill Sans.

Printed in China through Worldprint Ltd.

11 12 13 14 15   10 9 8 7 6 5 4 3 2 1

PHOTOGRAPH ACKNOWLEDGEMENTS

The British Library Board, pages 6 (Cotton MS Tiberius C.II, f5v.), 12 (top: Cotton Augustus ii 29), 52 (Cotton MS Vespasian A.i, f30b), 64 (Harley Roll Y. 6 roundel 9); Canterbury Archaeological Trust Ltd, pages 11 (bottom), 21, 24 (drawn by John Atherton Bowen), 38 (bottom), 45, 67 (bottom); English Heritage Photo Library, pages 4 (Peter Dunn, English Heritage Graphics Team), 14, 58 (Peter Dunn, English Heritage Graphics Team), 60 (bottom); Graham Norrie, page 55; The Institute of Archaeology, Oxford, pages 12 (bottom), 27, 31 (bottom), 41, 57 (bottom), 69 (bottom); By permission of the National Trust, photos by Sally Crawford, pages 28 (bottom), 37 (bottom), 55 (top); Oxford Archaeology Ltd, illustrated by Peter Lorimer, page 39; Regia Anglorum, www.regia.org, pages 17 (bottom), 23, 36 (top), 38 (top), 44 (top), 50 (top), 51 (top), 54 (top and bottom), 62 (bottom); St Edmundsbury Borough Council / West Stow Anglo-Saxon Village and Visitor Centre, photos by Sally Crawford, pages 9, 10, 17 (top), 18 (top), 19 (top and bottom), 20, 22, 28 (top), 29, 30 (top and bottom), 31 (top), 32, 40, 42 (bottom), 43 (top), 56 (bottom), 61, 67 (top), 68; Tony Randall, pages 8 (bottom), 18 (bottom), 35, 36 (bottom), 37 (top), 42 (top), 44 (bottom), 48, 49, 50 (bottom), 69 (top). Original artwork © Dominic Andrews, pages 46–7. All other images from author's collection.

DEDICATION
For Tony Randall.

COVER IMAGE:

A reconstruction drawing of the royal palace complex at Yeavering as it might have appeared in the early seventh century. In the foreground is a totem or ceremonial beam and droveway for cattle. The amphitheatre lies beyond the hall complex.(©English Heritage Photo Library: Peter Dunn, English Heritage Graphics Team)

Shire Publications is supporting the Woodland Trust, the UK's leading woodland conservation charity, by funding the dedication of trees.

Contents

PREFACE   4

INTRODUCTION   6

FAMILY   14

HOME AND NEIGHBOURHOOD   20

WORK   27

FOOD AND DRINK   34

SHOPPING AND STYLE   39

TRANSPORT   48

RELAXATION AND ENTERTAINMENT   52

EDUCATION AND SOCIAL SERVICE   58

HEALTH   64

PLACES TO VISIT   70

INDEX   72

PREFACE

THE FIRST CENTURIES after the departure of the Romans in AD 410 used to seem so obscure they were known as the Dark Ages. Their importance was never in doubt – these years saw the arrival from the Continent of the Anglo-Saxons, who established many of the towns and villages we still inhabit, and whose language forms the basis of our own. Yet they were mostly illiterate, and little was known of how they lived – at least until the return of Christianity at the end of the sixth century.

All this has changed remarkably in recent years, thanks to the patient and fascinating contribution of archaeology. Anglo-Saxon archaeology has always offered some spectacular remains – the Sutton Hoo ship burial, found in Suffolk in the 1930s, showed how a great king was buried and yielded many fine artefacts; while other discoveries were more prosaic yet probably told us more of how people lived and died. Both types of find have continued in recent years – with the equally spectacular hoard of some 1,500 items from the early seventh century found by a metal detectorist buried in a field in Staffordshire in 2009. Advances in biochemical, DNA and other technical analysis have produced a great deal of new information about disease, food and lifestyle which was unavailable to earlier generations of scholars.

As a result, much of the darkness of the Dark Ages has been dispelled, and many living history groups have enthusiastically added their own practical knowledge of ways of living.

Sally Crawford, a practising archaeologist, has skilfully drawn together all this knowledge to present a fresh picture of the men and women who took over the old Roman province and established their own very different civilisation among its ruins. It was a civilisation that produced some enduring achievements – the epic of Beowulf, the wondrously complex patterns of the Lindisfarne gospels and the great craftsmanship of the Sutton Hoo treasures among them.

Peter Furtado
General Editor

Opposite:
A reconstruction of the early-seventh-century royal ship burial at Mound I, Sutton Hoo.

5

Incipit
liber primus
ecclesiastice historiae
gentis anglorum

Brittania oceani insula cui quondam
Albion nomen fuit inter septentrionem et occidentem
locata est, Germaniae Galliae
Hispaniae maximis Europae partibus
multo intervallo adversa.

Quae per milia passuum octingenta in bo-
reum longe latitudinis habet,
ccc. excepta dum tractuum prolixi-
oribus diversorum promonto-
riorum tractibus.

quibus efficitur ut circuitus eius
quadragies octies lxxv milia
compleat. habet a meridie Galliam
Belgicam cuius proximum litus
transmeantibus aperit civitas
dictum Rutubi portus.

A tergo autem unde oceano infinito
patet, orcades insulas habet
optimae purissimis atque arbor
insulae...

INTRODUCTION

THE BEGINNINGS of Anglo-Saxon society in England are extremely difficult to pin down exactly, because the fifth century, during which a Romano-British way of life and culture was replaced by an Anglo-Saxon one, is a century with almost no written sources, and very few surviving visible remains.

In the centuries before the Anglo-Saxon arrival, Romano-British culture was characterised by a belief in Christianity, by villas and towns, and by contact with the wider Roman world. At some point before the fifth century, this way of life began to collapse. Late Romano-British settlements have few coins, stone villa buildings fell into disrepair and were replaced by wooden structures, and examples of late Romano-British pottery vessels show signs of having been repaired when they broke, rather than being discarded and replaced.

According to contemporary documentary sources, the Romano-British people recognised that their economically straitened circumstances, together with the recall of the Roman armies from Britain, left them vulnerable to attack from neighbouring kingdoms and pirates. One of the threats was the groups of barbarians from the northern seaboard of Europe and Scandinavia – the Germanic tribes who came to settle in England. Because their descendents assumed that most of the settlers were Anglians, from the Angeln area of Germany, or Saxons, from Saxony in Germany, the new people became known as the 'Anglo-Saxons'. The threat posed by these groups is reflected in the series of defensive structures, known as the Saxon shore forts, constructed from the third century, built to protect the south-eastern and southern coast of England from attack.

By the first half of the fifth century, archaeological evidence suggests that Anglo-Saxon culture was already finding its way into England. It is not certain how many Germanic migrants came to England, or why they came. Gildas, a British monk writing in the sixth century about the disaster of the Anglo-Saxon arrival, thought of their

Opposite: The opening of Book I of Bede's *The Ecclesiastical History of the English People*, composed at Jarrow and completed in AD 731.

Above: Burgh castle, Norfolk; one of the shore forts built by the Romans to protect the coast from Saxons.

coming in terms of an invasion. He recorded that they were invited in by a 'proud tyrant' leader of the Romano-British, to act as mercenaries to protect the leader and his people, but instead, seeing the weakness of the people and the richness of the land, they turned on their employers and, after numerous battles, succeeded in driving the British out of lowland England. Later Anglo-Saxons, like the scholarly Bede (AD 673–735), a monk at Jarrow, also recorded a version of this story as part of the 'history' of his people.

The simple story of invasions, battles and the driving out of the Romano-British has been challenged. It is possible that the newcomers were economic migrants or refugees from the Continent, where, amongst other problems, rising sea levels were flooding some of the coastal settlements. It is also possible that many of the Romano-British, rather than being driven out of the country or enslaved by warlike Anglo-Saxons, instead adopted an Anglo-Saxon way of life, becoming, to all intents and purposes, Anglo-Saxon.

Detail from a
sixth-century
cremation urn
from West Stow,
Suffolk.

By the early sixth century, the settlements, cemeteries and types
of objects used in most of lowland England can be characterised as
'Anglo-Saxon'. Though there are regional variations, the objects,
graves and the remains of buildings associated with England from the
sixth to the seventh centuries are identifiable as belonging to the
people who regarded themselves as being descended from the
Germanic tribes who had conquered the British and ruled England.
As far as we can tell, they spoke a common language – now known as
Old English – and identified themselves as different from their
predecessors in the land (the British) and different from other groups
living in the British Isles (the Picts and the Irish) – as well as the
Germanic groups who dominated the parts of Europe closest to
England, particularly the powerful Merovingian Franks of France, and
the Frisians further north, who were known for their trading and
seafaring skills.

The eighth-century monk, Bede, recounted that those who
settled in England came from distinct parts of the Continent – the
people who settled around East Anglia and Lincolnshire were from
Angeln in what is now Germany, those who settled in Kent were
Jutes from Jutland, and those who settled in central England were
from Saxony. Although Bede's account of the traditional origin of
the Anglo-Saxon tribes appears to have been a very simplified
version of a much more complicated pattern of migration and
settlement, the archaeological evidence supports the idea of strong

Opposite page,
bottom: Dyke
Hills, Dorchester-
on-Thames. Lying
just outside the
Roman town of
Dorchester, this
Iron Age rampart
was the site of an
early Germanic
'mercenary'
burial.

local, tribal identities existing in England before the seventh century, shown by regional costumes and jewellery styles for women, and regional variation in burial ritual.

There is also some evidence to show that links with the old homelands were maintained in some areas after the arrival of Anglo-Saxon culture in England. In other ways, however, Anglo-Saxon archaeology is distinctive, and some aspects of Continental life – in particular the layout of settlements and the structure of Continental hall buildings incorporating animal byres – seem not to have been copied in England.

Evidence for the fifth to seventh centuries in Anglo-Saxon England is essentially based on the archaeological remains. Early Anglo-Saxon settlements were first identified in the 1920s by the archaeologist E. T. Leeds, but, compared with the grander structures left by the Romano-British, the traces of Anglo-Saxon settlement were disappointing. Anglo-Saxons of this period used wood rather than stone for their buildings, and as a result, their settlements are only identifiable by post-holes, pits and ditches in the ground. The most prolific finds of this period come from the cemeteries, because Anglo-Saxons practised burial with grave goods and grave furniture. The huge range and variety of grave goods burnt on funeral pyres or placed in the ground with inhumation graves suggests that the Anglo-Saxons were generally

The reconstructed Anglo-Saxon village at West Stow, built on the site of a fifth- to seventh-century Anglo-Saxon settlement.

wealthy enough to be able to dedicate a considerable surplus to the dead, permanently removing brooches, weapons, vessels, clothing and food from circulation amongst the living.

As the sixth century went on, the idea of kingship developed, and as successful leaders extended their territories, Anglo-Saxon society began to change. Hierarchies of power were expressed more clearly in the settlements and cemeteries, and the most powerful kings of new kingdoms such as Wessex, Mercia, East Anglia, Bernicia and Deira began to seek useful marriage alliances with rival dynasties and Continental and British kings.

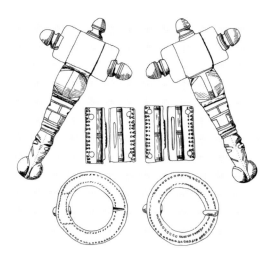

Iron brooches and wrist clasps typical of fifth- and sixth-century female dress fittings from Anglian areas of England.

By the end of the sixth century (and quite possibly associated with the rise of kingship in Anglo-Saxon England), Christian missionaries began to have an impact on the pagan Anglo-Saxons. What we know of this time suggests that, in some districts, pockets of British Christianity had held on; but, at least according to Bede, there was no love lost between the British Christians and the Anglo-Saxons, and Bede accused the British Christians of making no effort to convert their pagan Anglo-Saxon neighbours. Bede did not have much to say, however, in his most well-known book, *The Ecclesiastical History of the*

Seventh-century burial from the cemetery at Buckland, Dover. This wealthy adult female's grave includes gold bracteates and colourful beads at her neck, the remains of a pouch at her waist, and imported glass at her feet.

The only surviving East Saxon charter is written in Latin and dates to AD 686–688. It is a grant by Aethelred, kinsman of King Sebbi, to Abbess Aethelburh of Barking.

A disc brooch buried with a female from Updown, Kent.

English People, about events in the Midlands and in neighbouring Wales – it may be that some conversions did take place as a result of interaction with the British in these areas.

Irish missionaries, including Aidan from AD 635, began converting the English, having a particular impact on the northern kingdoms. Further south, Frankish missionaries attempted to convert the pagan Anglo-Saxons, too – the most well known of these is probably the Burgundian St Felix (d. 647), who became the first Bishop of the East Angles. The most important missionary effort, however, was inspired by Pope Gregory the Great, who, according to Bede, saw Anglo-Saxon slaves for sale in the market of Rome and decided to convert these pagan people on the edge of the known world. In 597, a missionary party sent by Gregory, led by St Augustine, made landfall in Kent and was welcomed by King Aethelbert and his Christian Frankish wife, Bertha. Kent converted to Christianity, and one by one, with some backsliding, the other kings and kingdoms followed suit.

With Christianity came significant changes to the Anglo-Saxon landscape. Churches and monasteries were built, and, while some of them were built of timber, the traditional building material, new stone churches were also erected from the outset. Stonemasons and glaziers were brought from the Continent to teach their skills to the English, and other new skills were introduced with Christianity too, in particular writing and reading. From the seventh century onwards, the elite, at least, had access to literacy, and, although the majority of the documentary sources for Anglo-Saxon England belong to the later period, some manuscripts do survive from this period. Some of the documentary sources, even if not quite contemporary with this period, shed some light on early Anglo-Saxon England. Particularly useful are *The Ecclesiastical History of the English People*, written by Bede, and the later *Anglo-Saxon Chronicle*, which brought together Anglo-Saxon records of the history of England. Surviving Old English law codes, wills, charters, medical texts and poetry, even when not contemporary with the pre-Viking period in England, do help to flesh out the archaeological evidence.

With the development of kingdoms, the conversion to Christianity, and new, strong links with the wider Christian world, England in the eighth century was a relatively rich, prosperous society with schools, taxes, trading centres, mints, laws and ecclesiastical centres. A social hierarchy had developed, with kings and aristocrats at the top, and slaves at the bottom, with various classes of free and unfree people in between. Most people were still involved in agricultural activities, but resources – fields, water sources, woodlands and quarries – were controlled by the church and the elite, who developed large estates. Anglo-Saxon England was relatively quiet – wars between kingdoms broke out in times of uncertain succession to the throne, when ambitious kings tried to accumulate more power – but on the whole, crops sown in the spring would be harvested in the autumn. Anglo-Saxon England offered easy pickings for the Vikings, who arrived on the holy island of Lindisfarne in AD 793, sacking and looting the monastery, and sending shock waves through the whole of Christian Europe. Politically, culturally and ethnically, the Viking invasions marked a change in Anglo-Saxon England, and it is at this point that the chronological spread of this book ends.

A late-eighth-century cross shaft from Bewcastle, Cumbria, decorated with animal ornament and figural scenes, including here a falconer in the lower panel, possibly St John the Evangelist. The cross-shaft incorporates runic script containing a number of personal names.

FAMILY

THE IMPORTANCE of family in early Anglo-Saxon England is hard to overstate. Early villages consisted of family units. Everyone knew everyone else. Who you were related to, and how you were related to them, was central to your place in society. When the warrior Beowulf arrived at the hall of King Hrothgar, according to the Old English poem, his very first task was to establish his credentials by stating clearly who he was related to – who his father was, and whose family he belonged to.

Family was important because your family guaranteed your security. In a society without police, laws were upheld and order was maintained through social pressure and family networks. To be caught in a crime was to bring your family – not just your immediate siblings and parents, but also your wider family of aunts, uncles and cousins – into disrepute. This is, at least, the implication of the earliest law codes. Equally, if you needed witnesses to support you, a man who could draw on a family known for its reputation and wealth was well on his way to being declared innocent.

It is hard to work out how familial bonds were created in Old English society. The earliest law codes suggest that a marriage was a contract which required the agreement of both families. Early laws were particularly keen to avoid the abduction of a woman before her marriage. Part of the marriage process involved the giving of a gift – *morgengifu* in Old English – to the bride from the groom or his family. This gift became the property of the wife. She could use this gift without interference, and, in later law codes, it is hers to bequest as she wanted. The *morgengifu* gave Anglo-Saxon married women economic independence.

The status of children depended to an extent on the nature of the relationship that resulted in their birth. If they were born of parents who had contracted a public marriage, then both the father's and the mother's family would have obligations of care to the child;

Opposite: Artist's reconstruction of the early Anglo-Saxon village at Mucking, Essex, showing timber halls and satellite buildings.

where the parents had not made a public contract with the agreement of their families, then the father could refuse to acknowledge the child.

It was important, however, that ties of obligation to children extended beyond the immediate family because, as the archaeological evidence indicates, life expectancy was not high in early Anglo-Saxon England – perhaps thirty years on average for men and women if they survived the first five years of life – and it was crucial that an orphaned child had relatives who would feel honour bound to maintain the child and vouch for it as it grew up. The underlying fear of leaving a child without protection and family may be the simplest explanation for the practice of fosterage, which seems to have been important in early medieval society as a whole. Fosterage extended the range of an individual's contacts in case of future difficulties. If a child was fostered, foster parents had the same legal and social responsibilities for a child as its biological parents, and foster siblings also had important bonds of honour and obligation.

Female brooch sets from Kent. The style and shape of the brooches indicated tribal or regional affiliations.

The skeletal evidence from the cemeteries sometimes indicates a considerable investment of care in some sick children who survived congenital illnesses and lived to adulthood. Some burials also indicate strong bonds of affection between carers and children, for example in grave goods given to children, which went beyond the usual formalities

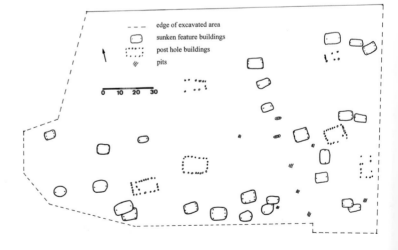

edge of excavated area
sunken feature buildings
post hole buildings
pits

0 10 20 30

Simplified plan of part of the excavated area at West Stow, Suffolk, showing the sprawling layout of huts, buildings and halls; scale in metres.

A reconstruction of a sunken-featured building from West Stow Anglo-Saxon village. Experiments at the site show that such huts could be viable for at least twenty-five years.

of laying out the body for the burial ritual. Given the relatively short life expectancy, it is not perhaps surprising that grandparents, in the documentary sources, did not often play an important part in the lives of their grandchildren. Instead, bonds between brothers and sisters were often recorded as being of significance in Old English documentary sources, and the bonds of loyalty and responsibility between a man and his sister's son were particularly powerful.

The names given to children also reinforced family ties, at least amongst the elite, where alliterative naming was common. For example, the father of Coenwulf of Mercia (d. 821) was Cuthbert, his grandfather was Bassa, and his great-grandfather was Cynreow. Coenwulf's brothers were Cuthred and Ceolwulf, and his children were called Cenelm, Cwenthryth and Burgenhild. This branch of the family had strong alliteration in 'C' names, with a secondary alliteration with 'B'.

Old English names were often composed of two elements, such as 'cuth' [famous] and 'red' [counsel] to make 'Cuthred', and both boys and girls would be given names with similar elements. St Hilda of Whitby's father was Hereric ('ruler of battle/army'), and her sister was Hereswith ('strong battle/army'). Royal girls like Hereswith and Hilda were given names, like the boys, that were full of images of war and battle. Even apparently gentler names, such as Frideswide ('great peace'), reference the role of royal princesses as tools in

Ceremonial activities reinforced family bonds and community identity.

complicated dynastic strategies – the marriage of a princess might secure peace between warring kingdoms.

How families occupied the villages of the early period is difficult to assess. Anglo-Saxon buildings yield little information about function, internal layout and household activities. The majority of buildings appear to have consisted of a single room, though partitions made of cloth are possible. Village buildings were single storey, though by the seventh century, the largest hall buildings may have had a second floor level. Privacy must have been a rare commodity in Anglo-Saxon home life. In the later sixth century, there is evidence for the addition of a small chamber at one end of building, with exits to the main room and to the outside. Perhaps these little rooms served as entrance porches, providing some separation between the family and visitors to

A key from a female burial at West Stow, Suffolk. Keys were associated with women's costumes, and would be hung from a belt at the waist.

Eighth-century sculpture from the church at Breedon on the Hill. The church provided an alternative for women who wanted to avoid marriage, but many churches were family-run affairs.

the house. Larger buildings also developed internal annexes at this time. The purpose of these annexes is not known, but again, it is possible that they functioned as separate chambers – perhaps sleeping areas – giving the family privacy from slaves, servants or other dependents; but the similarity of these chambers to the square chancels of churches offers the possibility that these annexes served as private chapels or shrines. The central post in the square annexe of a building at the high-status site of Cowdery's Down, Hampshire, supports the idea that these structures were spaces for domestic shrines.

Above: A reconstructed interior of a hall with a central, raised hearth. Stake holes in excavated buildings indicate possible screens to separate sleeping areas, as shown here at the West Stow Anglo-Saxon village.

Right: A reconstructed locking mechanism on a door. A long key pushed through the hole could be manipulated to lift the latch.

HOME AND
NEIGHBOURHOOD

A view of the reconstructed village, West Stow. Houses were built to take the best advantage of sunlight through doors on the long walls, but otherwise show little sign of a controlled or planned layout.

EARLY ANGLO-SAXON life, for most people, revolved around their home and neighbouring fields, woodlands, rivers and water sources. Excavated Anglo-Saxon settlements, such as West Stow in Suffolk and Mucking in Essex, show that community life centred on the timber-built halls, which were the setting for feasting, drinking and meetings. Satellite buildings – known as sunken-featured buildings because of the pits in their floors – were where day-to-day working and living took place. It is in the sunken-featured buildings that

Evidence for a Saxon building with post-holes from the Longmarket site in Canterbury.

evidence for pottery making, bone working, textile working and smithing is found. A typical village consisted of about three main halls, and perhaps ten to fifteen associated sunken-featured buildings. A curiosity of early Anglo-Saxon settlements is their lack of boundaries. Apart from some fences – which appear to have been used to enclose animals – early Anglo-Saxon settlements do not have boundary ditches or fences. They do not have defences, and the inhabitants of the villages did not feel the need to fence or ditch the spaces around their houses. This also suggests that cattle were let out to pasture on open fields at a distance from the village.

Woodlands provided an important resource. Timber was useful for building and for fuel, but woodlands also provided a habitat for the wild animals that supplemented the Anglo-Saxon diet, as well as pannage for pigs, which would forage for food such as acorns, chestnuts and beechnuts. Recent carbon and nitrogen isotope analysis of early Anglo-Saxon human bones has indicated that pigs played a much more important part in the diet than surviving animal-bone evidence from settlements would suggest (the analysis also suggests that chickens, almost absent from the archaeological record, also played an important part in the diet). The importance of woodland as a resource is indicated by a law of King Ine (d. 726) which declares that 'anyone who destroys a tree in a wood by fire … shall pay 60 shillings, because fire is a thief'. Pannage was such an important resource that laws were required to protect it. According to Ine, anyone who persistently found someone else's pigs in his forest was owed six shillings, though if the pigs had only been there once or twice, the fine was only one or two shillings.

All known Anglo-Saxon houses were built of timber. Settlements show little sign of showing any overriding organisation – buildings are not lined up with each other, and there is no evidence for marked-out building plots. Land, it would seem, was a communal commodity. The fact that, when halls and sunken-featured buildings reached the end of their use, they were abandoned and replaced by new buildings erected elsewhere in the village, rather than being rebuilt, indicates that these early settlers were not pressed for space. The Anglo-Saxon habit of abandoning old structures and putting up new buildings in a fresh space has led to a phenomenon known as the 'wandering settlement'. Early Anglo-Saxon settlements would track across the landscape over time, sometimes moving considerable distances from the area of initial settlement.

Some fences were constructed on early Anglo-Saxon settlements, as here at the reconstructed village at West Stow, Suffolk, to keep animals away from the houses. Isotope analysis of pig bones suggest that some animals were living close to houses and were consuming the same food as humans.

With the emergence of kingdoms, however, tribal leaders and their followers felt the need to express their power through larger structures and bigger settlements. In the fifth to the sixth centuries, Anglo-Saxon settlements all share similar characteristics, but by the seventh and eighth centuries, there were more types of settlement, with the development of elite sites. The site of Chalton in Hampshire is a good example of one of these mid-Anglo-Saxon elite sites. The site plan shows fences marking out areas around buildings, and the buildings themselves show more order and alignment. Fences for paddocks and associated droveways also begin to appear. The fences indicate marked-out territory, but also a wider change in the use of land, because they suggest that animals, in particular cattle, were now being kept closer to the settlements, at least at some times of the year. More organised estates and growing specialism in production also led to the expansion of arable production.

The combination of greater organisation, and a change in land use around settlements, is exemplified by the excavated settlement at Quarrington, Lincolnshire. This site appears to have gone out of use by the ninth century, but in its mid-Saxon phase, three timber buildings were constructed, associated with three ditches running east–west at regular intervals, marking out evenly sized parcels of land, and perhaps acting as animal enclosures or paddocks.

The largest mid-Saxon halls were substantial structures – the biggest hall at Chalton is over 15 metres long. Opinions vary as to whether, on the basis of the surviving archaeological remains, the larger halls had two floors or only one, but either way they would

A reconstructed long hall. Halls were a focus for community activities, including feasting and storytelling. Halls became larger from the seventh century, as kings and aristocrats used them to signal their growing power and status.

have been imposing. The later poetic descriptions of Anglo-Saxon royal halls suggest they would have been covered in elaborate carvings, perhaps painted, and the interiors, with soaring timber ceilings, would have been decorated with tapestries on the walls. At Catholme in Staffordshire, a site established in the late sixth or early seventh century provides evidence for a new attitude towards buildings, which show signs of maintenance and repair. The settlement here consisted of enclosed farmsteads, and it may be that, with the parcelling out of land, domestic space, and the buildings associated with that space, became hereditary and came to be viewed as a permanent part of the landscape. How far this parcelling out of the land indicates control and lordship, and how far it represents organisation at a local, community level, is still a matter for debate.

Several Anglo-Saxon palace sites of this period are known through aerial photography. One has been excavated – the site of Yeavering in Northumberland. Yeavering is mentioned by Bede as the place where the powerful King Edwin and his retinue listened to the missionary Paulinus, accepted Christianity, and were baptised in the nearby river. Traces of a unique amphitheatre at the site, with the seats facing a central performance area marked by a timber beam, indicate gathering and display. A huge earthen enclosure indicates a large corral for cattle –

An artist's reconstruction of Canterbury in c. AD 600 showing the Anglo-Saxon settlement sprawling within the framework of the decayed Roman town.

perhaps cattle brought to the king as tribute. Several buildings have ritual features, including one with a floor made up of ox bones, and another where – unusually for the time – an old timber-framed building had been enclosed by a later, second timber structure. It is speculated that this building may have been an early church, since it appears that only with the building of churches did particular spaces in settlements become special, requiring buildings to be rebuilt on the same spot.

The majority of Roman towns were abandoned through the fifth and sixth centuries, or occupation continued in them only as squatter occupation. The archaeology of this period in most of the Roman towns in England is characterised by a layer of black earth, made up of organic material as former streets were returned to agricultural sites. Where walls stood, gateways in the walls still directed traffic so that relics of the main north–south and east–west roads remained, but excavations at Roman towns such as London and Canterbury show early Anglo-Saxon inhabitants widening the former road as their carts and animals tracked over old street boundaries.

Some Roman cities kept a memory of their old importance as church sites – when Augustine arrived in Kent he was directed to the church of St Martin's for services, so the function of the Roman building was still recognised. After conversion, Anglo-Saxon kings used old Roman towns as their centres of power, reusing Roman

Escomb Church, County Durham, was founded in c. AD 670–675, and is one of the oldest Anglo-Saxon churches in England. Much of the building material for it came from the nearby Roman fort at Binchester. Apart from the addition of some medieval windows and the alteration of the south doorway, the church stands much as it was built.

One of the interlace panels from the cross shaft at Bewcastle, Cumbria. Similarly elaborate ornaments probably decorated timber buildings of the period.

churches. This pattern is visible, for example, at Canterbury, Winchester, York and London. But Roman towns were not where newly powerful kings wanted to locate their markets. To control (and tax) the exchange of goods in and out of their kingdoms, mid-Saxon kings established new places known as 'wic' sites.

Several 'wic' sites have been excavated, at London, Ipswich, York and Southampton. The Southampton 'wic', known as 'Hamwic', offers a good insight into this new form of settlement. It was located on the west bank of the River Itchen, as a new foundation, quite separate from an old Roman town further north. The settlement was constructed in around AD 700, with a planned, regularly laid-out pattern of streets in a grid, covering about 45 hectares. Houses were built of timber, and the site was densely occupied.

WORK

THERE IS SOME EVIDENCE that tasks were allotted according to age and gender, but above all to rank. It is no surprise that the skeletons in the cemeteries showing the highest levels of trauma in their life course – those with fractures, some of which may have been the result of violence – are also those which exhibit some levels of malnutrition in their skeletons. The hardest labour was carried out by slaves.

Later Anglo-Saxon documentary evidence suggests that there were a number of ways in which people became slaves. The first, and perhaps the most common, was to be captured, either by pirates raiding the coast of England, or through warfare. Poverty also drove people to slavery. Early law codes indicate that there was a requirement for slave owners to provide basic food, clothing and shelter for their slaves, and there were punishments for failing to do so. A lower-class freeman and his family suffering from poor harvests might well choose to sell themselves into slavery as a guarantee of survival – a better option than starving to death. Impoverished, desperate or greedy parents might also choose to sell their children into slavery. Slavery did not have to be a permanent state. There is some evidence to show that social mobility was a possibility in Anglo-Saxon society. According to the law codes, a slave could accumulate wealth, and might be able to buy their freedom, or might be granted their freedom by their owners.

Different types of craft industry were important in early Anglo-Saxon society. Pottery was an important material for cooking and storage vessels. Although the

A healed fracture to the arm of an adult male buried at Worthy Park, Kings Worthy, Hampshire. The bone was not set before healing, and the injury would have been permanently disabling.

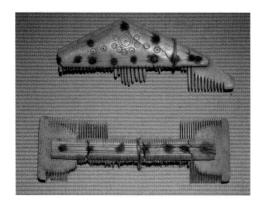

Worked bone combs from West Stow, Suffolk. Animal bone provided the raw material for many everyday items from combs to toggles and needles.

Romano-British had the technology to produce wheel-thrown pots, early Anglo-Saxon pottery was handmade and fired at relatively low temperatures. Anglo-Saxons did not use glazes either, which meant that their pottery had a limited use for liquids, but some pottery was decorated with stamps or combs to make repeating patterns before firing. Pottery was also used as a container for the ashes of the dead after cremation.

In the eighth century, pottery began to be mass-produced at industrial centres, fired in more sophisticated kilns. This pottery was coil-made on a slow wheel. The most important of these centres was the pottery industry at Ipswich, the wic site supporting the kingdom of East Anglia. Pottery kilns have been excavated at Ipswich, and the huge output of the kilns is illustrated by the distribution of the pottery, which has been found at sites as far afield as Oxfordshire to the west, Kent to the south and Yorkshire to the north. Away from East Anglia, this characteristic pottery is only found in association with high-status sites, showing how much this product was valued, though locally it was common. The pottery kilns at Ipswich are located in a small area to the north-east of the middle Anglo-Saxon settlement, and it has been suggested that this pottery industry was set up by immigrants from the Continent, who may well have established an enclave from

An early handmade pot from Suffolk. Pots like these served as containers, but were not glazed and were of limited use in food storage and cooking.

which to exploit their knowledge and technological ability.

Woodworking must have been a key activity on Anglo-Saxon settlements. Wood was one of the most important resources for Anglo-Saxon production, used for constructing all domestic buildings throughout the period, for heating, furniture, carts and ships. Large quantities of timber were required to produce the charcoal needed to smelt metal ores and fire pottery kilns. To this end, woodlands were valued and carefully managed resources, but wood has a very poor survival rate in the archaeological record for Anglo-Saxon England. The wooden coffin in which St Cuthbert's body was placed is perhaps the best surviving example of early Anglo-Saxon woodworking. Worked bone and antler have survived more plentifully, however,

A reconstruction of a vertical weaving loom at West Stow. Two women would have worked at one loom, and some weaving sheds held up to three looms, so weaving sheds were places for women to socialise as well as work.

and again, the examples suggest that even utilitarian items such as spindle whorls and bone combs might be beautifully decorated.

Bone as a material has survived in the form of boxes, knife handles, strap ends, clothing toggles, gaming pieces, pins, needles, keys and pottery stamps. Some of these artefacts – pottery stamps, for example – required only limited effort to create, but the skill and abilities of Anglo-Saxon boneworkmanship are exhibited in objects like the early-eighth-century Franks Casket, carved from whalebone. Some Anglo-Saxon bonework debris from the settlement sites shows that highly skilled work was not restricted to the elite. At the early Anglo-Saxon settlement of West Stow, Suffolk, for example, delicate bone combs were recovered, decorated with patterns that would have required the use of fine saws, drills, hammers and tools. Horn cores and wasters from middle Anglo-Saxon wic settlements indicate that bone working was one of the specialised industries of these production centres.

In the early Anglo-Saxon period, most women were probably involved in the production of textiles, which would have taken up a large percentage of their time. By the mid-Saxon period, however, rural

Anglo-Saxon loom weights were made of clay. Rarely decorated, they have been found in situ in excavations of early Anglo-Saxon settlements.

estates had weaving workshops where low-status women produced textiles for the estate's dependents. The metal 'weaving battens' found occasionally in wealthy women's graves, made of pattern-welded steel, and sometimes made from recycled sword blades, may have indicated a higher-ranking woman in charge of estate textile production.

The bones from the early Anglo-Saxon settlement site at Lechlade include a high proportion of cattle, and a leather worker's awl was

A reconstruction of an Anglo-Saxon kiln at West Stow, Suffolk.

An iron shield boss decorated with gilt studs from a male grave. High-quality metalwork was produced by Anglo-Saxon smiths.

found in male grave 57, suggesting that leather was also an important community product. The striking number of calf bones in the archaeological deposits from the settlement at Lechlade suggest that the community was producing surplus cattle, which were being used to produce beef and leather, and perhaps also vellum – it has been estimated that the production of a book like the *Lindisfarne Gospels*, for example, would have required one thousand five hundred calf skins.

A two-strand necklace with gold bracteates, gold, silver, garnet and glass beads from a grave at Finglesham. This wealthy woman was also buried with a bone comb, a glass claw beaker, silver brooches, a copper bowl, a pouch, and an iron weaving sword.

Perhaps in the seventh and eighth centuries, places like Lechlade were beginning to specialise in the production of leather or vellum to supply an increasingly literate elite, as well as producing surplus material. Such trade might explain the wealth of the community, demonstrated in the high-status, exotic artefacts found in some of the graves, including high-status weaponry, gold and garnet jewellery, cowrie shells and amethysts.

Few, if any, people lived in stone houses, but many would have had the experience of worshipping in churches built of stone, and a significant number of people were engaged in quarrying, transporting, building and sculpting in stone. Romano-British towns and villas were a useful source of building material, and a number of Anglo-Saxon churches incorporated recycled material (*spolia*) in their construction. Stone quarries were also exploited in the Anglo-Saxon period, especially where stone lay close to the surface. A limestone outcrop in Stonegrave, North Yorkshire, for example, was quarried from at least the Roman period, and it is no coincidence that in the eighth century, a religious house at the site was recorded with the place name, which means 'stone hole' in Old English.

Scale from smithing, clay deposits and finds of loom weights and spinning equipment suggest that the sunken-featured buildings were the focus for craft activity in the early Anglo-Saxon settlements.

Iron ore for making metal could be found as bog iron, or in surface deposits as haematite or carbonate iron ores, which were exploited at a variety of locations, such as the Weald, Lincolnshire, the Forest of Dean and Northamptonshire. A few early Anglo-Saxon settlements, such as Mucking, Essex have produced evidence of slag, suggesting some iron-smelting took place within settlements, though nothing to match the scale of iron-smelting in contemporary Scandinavia, for example. The iron ore was smelted into iron by heating it to a high temperature in a shaft over a pit, for which huge amounts of charcoal would have been required. The end product was a mix of iron and slag, known as bloom, which required further heating and hammering before it would produce iron. Much more common in early Anglo-Saxon settlement sites is evidence of hammer-scale: the by-product of hammer-welding hot iron, suggesting domestic working of iron bloom (and a trade in iron bars), perhaps to make the ubiquitous iron knives. Analysis of early Anglo-Saxon weaponry, however, suggests that much of the smithing showed great expertise, and might have been the work of a dedicated specialist smith. Spearheads are the most common weapons found in graves. Usually, they were forged from a single piece of metal, with the socket flattened and folded to form an open tube into which the shaft could be inserted. Some spearheads were more complex, however: one seventh-century example from Broom Hill Quarry, Sandy, Bedfordshire, was made out of four pieces of iron with different properties, welded together to create a decorative pattern on the socket blade.

Pattern welding was a technique particularly exploited by specialist Anglo-Saxon smiths to create highly prized pattern-welded swords. The technique involved repeatedly folding and hammer-welding a bar of iron to build up a tough layered structure. Strips of this steel were then twisted and hammered together, so that, when polished, they created a pattern of twisted lines along the length of the blade, an appearance memorably described by the *Beowulf* poet as *atertanum fah*, 'made with poisoned stripes'.

A seventh-century cemetery find from Tattershall Thorpe, Lincolnshire, has provided us with information about the tools associated with smithing. During the excavation of the cemetery, a grave, located at a distance from any other burials, contained two deposits of metalworking tools and other materials. The iron tools include an anvil, hammers, tongs, a file, shears and punches. The hoard also included copper alloy and other metals, glass and organic remains. The hoard may be associated with a foreign (Frankish) artisan.

FOOD AND DRINK

THE CLIMATE in Anglo-Saxon England appears to have been milder and damper than it is in England today, and this is reflected in the crops that could be sown. In the opening paragraphs of his *Ecclesiastical History*, Bede particularly wrote about the good climate, fertility and abundance of the country he knew: 'the island is rich in crops and trees, and has good pasturage for cattle and beasts of burden. It also produces vines in certain districts, and has plenty of both land- and waterfowl of various kinds. It is remarkable too for its rivers, which abound in fish, particularly salmon and eels, and for copious springs...' On the whole, the archaeological evidence supports this picture of variety and abundance.

The majority of early Anglo-Saxon food and drink was produced locally. Isotope analysis of skeletons from excavated early Anglo-Saxon cemeteries suggests that the main diet consisted of chicken, pork, beef and lamb, supplemented by wild birds and some fish. With the rise of Christianity, fish became more prominent in the diet. Wheat, oats and barley were grown, and fruit and vegetables were seasonally available. Salt was widely used to flavour dishes. One characteristic of early Anglo-Saxon skeletons is their very good levels of dental health: there was very little sugar in the Anglo-Saxon diet. Honey was the only sweetener available in early medieval England. It was a valuable commodity, used to make the sweet alcoholic drink, mead.

The Anglo-Saxons arrived in a land that had been farmed for centuries before, and, though the evidence is not clear in all parts of the country, it would appear that, even though the Anglo-Saxons farmed less intensively than their Romano-British predecessors, they kept up pre-existing cultivated areas. The cultivated landscape of Roman Britain did not return to scrubland or wilderness. Where there was tree cover, the woodlands were almost certainly a carefully managed resource, rather than wild. Analysis of plant material at the early Anglo-Saxon settlement at West Stow, Suffolk showed that spelt, wheat, rye, barley and oats were all present. Spelt was cultivated in the Roman period, and seems to have persisted as a crop in early Anglo-Saxon Suffolk, but by the middle Saxon period, it no longer appears in the faunal record, suggesting that spelt had been replaced as a crop by other grain crops with higher yields.

Early English land units ('hides') probably reflected the area of land required to support one family (*hiwung*). A late Old English document, the *Rectitudines Singularum Personarum*, suggested that a '*cotsetle*' (cottager) required a minimum of five acres of land for subsistence, but the number of families supported by a single hide seems to have increased into the later Anglo-Saxon period, perhaps as a result of more intensive farming practices, and the size of a hide differed according to the resources and value of the land.

In addition to the wide range of foods and drinks available to early English communities, some people also had access to spices, herbs, wine and oils, fruit and nuts from abroad. Anglo-Saxon kingdoms had access to trade routes that stretched from the Baltic to the Indian Ocean, though these routes were sometimes disrupted by wars and bad weather. The rarity of imported items may have been one reason why they were included as ingredients in medical recipes, and there is no doubt that some exotic commodities had great value. The pottery bottle of wine from the Rhineland placed in the early seventh-century lavish burial at Mound 1, Sutton Hoo was there to emphasise the extravagance of the burial. An example of the imported herbs and spices available to a monk who never left his Northumbrian home is preserved in the will of Bede, who bequeathed lavender, aniseed, cinnamon, cloves, cumin, coriander, cardamom, galingale, ginger, liquorice, sugar and pepper to his fellow monks.

It has been suggested that, to some extent, Anglo-Saxon diet was determined by wealth and gender. It has been noted that males buried with weapons are generally taller than males buried without weaponry, suggesting a better diet for those of higher status. Famine, however, was a constant worry. The *Anglo-Saxon Chronicles* record years in which the population was struck by drought, cattle fever, or floods, and the crops failed. Desperate, starving people sold themselves and their children into slavery, or threw themselves off cliffs to end their misery, according to one (possibly exaggerated) account. Even in an ordinary year, there would be seasonal periods of

White Park cattle came to England with the Romans. Deposits of cattle bones in Anglo-Saxon settlements and cemeteries show that beef was a valued source of food. Oxen were also useful for pulling carts.

glut and famine. Early spring was a particularly difficult time, when the winter stores were running low, but new crops had not yet had a chance to grow. Later documentary sources suggest that this was the time of year when spring growth such as cress and nettles – and perhaps the shoots of ground elder, introduced to Britain as a food source by the Romans – would have been eaten, providing valuable sources of iron and vitamins.

Food preparation areas are difficult to find in Anglo-Saxon archaeology. At the high-status seventh-century site of Yeavering, a building with two hearths stood close to a complex of pits that were filled with bone fragments, mostly cattle bones, which showed signs of butchery. Perhaps the building was a kitchen. Bread, a staple of the diet, was baked either on a pan over a fire, in the ashes of a fire, or in an oven. Examples of Anglo-Saxon ovens are known from the archaeological evidence from the sixth century onwards, though it is difficult to prove that they were used for baking bread, but early documentary sources record bread ovens, such as that described in the early eighth-century *Life of Ceolfrith*, which describes how an oven was cleaned out before the loaves were put in it for baking.

The mainstay of Anglo-Saxon cooking was the stew, made in a cauldron or kettle suspended over a fire. In elite households,

Above: Most villages were self-sufficient in food and drink, but passing traders and temporary markets offered the chance of variety in the diet.

Left: Later medical recipes suggest that watercress (Old English *cærse*) was a valuable source of iron and vitamins. Watercress, shown here being cultivated at Ewelme, requires fresh, flowing shallow water. The place names Carswell and Cresswell both derive from Old English, marking such places.

a metal vessel would be used, but the earthenware crocks found on lower-status sites could also be used for stewing food and creating broths. Stewing was an economical way of preparing foods, particularly where the meat might have been dried, cured, or came from an older animal.

A reliable source of water was crucially important to the success of a settlement, and this concern is shown in the large number of

early Anglo-Saxon place names that state, often quite precisely, the location and type of local water supply: Winterbourne is the site of a seasonal stream; Chadwell is the site of a cold spring; Bedwell marks a place where water from a spring needs to be collected in a vessel or butt (Old English *byden*): Chalfont, Urchfont and Havant, all 'font' place names, are linked with Roman settlements with springs. Milk derived from cows, goats and sheep, as well as being used to make dairy products, was also a useful drink; one (fragmentary) late Anglo-Saxon will from Bury St Edmunds provided for four pence for milk at a funeral feast. The main beverages at feasts were ale, beer (probably derived from fermented fruits, like cider), mead and wine.

There is definite evidence for hops being used to make ale in Anglo-Saxon England by the tenth century. Anglo-Saxon 'beer' (*beor*) was a sweet, strong drink, made from fermented fruit.

The grave goods associated with the burial at Mound 1, Sutton Hoo in the early seventh century included a collection of objects symbolic of the role of the tribal leader as host and feast giver. These items range from local products to valuable exotic imports. Feasting equipment associated with this single burial included a large cauldron with a chain link to hang it from a roof beam, maple-wood drinking cups, silver bowls from Byzantium, decorated drinking horns, a pottery bottle containing wine imported from the Continent, wooden buckets including an iron-bound, yew-wood vat which has been estimated to have a capacity of about 178 pints, and two silver spoons. The presence of feasting equipment within this grave underlines how important food and feasting was within the Anglo-Saxon community. A meal was not simply a matter of taking on calories; it could also be an important communal act, conferring obligations on the guests, reinforcing social bonds, and providing an occasion for the discussion and

Reconstruction of the great cauldron in the grave at Mound 1, Sutton Hoo.

Above: Longhall interior.

Below: Glass communal drinking vessels from excavations at Buckland Anglo-Saxon cemetery; part of elite feasting and drinking tableware.

dissemination of important information. Food was used to convey messages about ethnic identity, status, religious affiliation, gender and occupation, as well as being used to reward followers, cement political and kinship relationships, and create and strengthen social bonds at feasts, marriages, funerals and other events.

Small, versatile, single-bladed iron knives are amongst the most common dress items found in association with Anglo-Saxon burials, and, apart from fingers and the occasional spoon, they were the sole eating utensil. While drinking vessels and food containers were probably shared at mealtimes, it is likely that diners used their own personal knives to cut, spear and transport their food to their mouths, and perhaps to pick their teeth, too.

At Castledyke, Humberside, twelve graves contained turned wooden bowls decorated with metal fittings. As well as having metal decorations, the bowls at Castledyke were made from a variety of woods, and at Sewerby, Yorkshire, bowls found in graves were made from wild cherry, ash, chestnut, maple and beech, suggesting that the appearance of bowls as decorative items was as important as their functional use.

Finds of glass on Anglo-Saxon settlement sites are rare. Excavations at the early Anglo-Saxon cemetery at Morningthorpe, Norfolk, recovered the remains of about 365 inhumation and nine cremation burials. Only one of these burials included a glass vessel. The excavations at the early Anglo-Saxon settlement of West Stow, Suffolk, produced only four fragments of brown glass, two of which certainly belonged to the same claw beaker. The scarcity of glass vessels in early Anglo-Saxon contexts suggests that precious few examples of imported glassware might be found in each community, though most people would have seen glass vessels.

SHOPPING AND STYLE

THERE IS GOOD EVIDENCE that early Anglo-Saxons traded their surplus produce in exchange for both locally made goods and more exotic materials from other geographical areas, even overseas, which were brought by passing traders. For the earliest Anglo-Saxon settlements, however, there is little evidence of specialist shops, or of anyone, apart from the itinerant merchants, who made a daily living from trading.

The early Anglo-Saxons, with their apparently modest living standards in small timber-built houses with a farming economy, did produce significant surpluses of goods in addition to their daily requirements, because they were able to place materials in graves or in funeral pyres to commemorate the dead. The early Anglo-Saxons did not have a coin economy, so evidence for trade comes from the distribution of artefacts, and the presence of items associated with trade, such as balances and weights. Scales and balance pans have been found in graves across England, though they are not common, and the majority of finds are concentrated in Kentish male graves. As the closest site to the wealthy Merovingian kingdom across the Channel, and as the first kingdom to convert to Christianity, it is hardly surprising that a thriving trade brought Continental goods to Kent, to be distributed from Kent to other parts of southern Britain, largely via river routes.

Although most scales and balance pans found to date were in the graves of males, women were also involved in trading. A woman at Castledyke, Humberside, was buried in a well-furnished grave with grave goods including a set of scales, and a woman

Reconstruction of the seasonal mid-Anglo-Saxon market excavated at Dorney Lake, Eton, Buckinghamshire.

Detail of a reconstructed sixth-century Anglo-Saxon female dress.

from Lechlade, Gloucestershire, had a pouch filled with uncut garnets placed by her body. The quantity of the stones suggests that they were intended for trade, rather than for her own use.

While Kent benefited from its closeness to France, and from the survival of centres of trade and Christianity such as Canterbury, other parts of Anglo-Saxon England also had long-distance contact with the Continent, and these contacts could be far-flung. Grave goods in the Mound 1 ship burial at Sutton Hoo originated in Ireland, Merovingian France, Scandinavia, Coptic Egypt, and India. Even before the development of the wic trading centres, men and women in Anglo-Saxon England had access to exotic goods. A feature of some sixth-century women's dress is their pouches, hung from bag-rings made of ivory.

One reason why Anglo-Saxon England traded with the Continent, even in the fifth and sixth centuries when England appeared to be a dangerous pagan country, was because the Anglo-Saxons had goods to offer, including hunting dogs and slaves. By the eighth century, Anglo-Saxon England also had an international reputation for the quality of its embroideries and cloths and for its manuscripts and scholarship.

With the establishment of wics and the introduction of a monetary economy in the late seventh and eighth centuries, Anglo-Saxons had the option of taking part in shopping. Visitors to the ports of England —York, London, Hamwic — were impressed by their lively trade, and by the busy mix of foreigners – craftspeople, sailors and traders – thronging the streets. Excavations at Hamwic, Lundenwic and Gyppeswic (Southampton, Aldwych and Ipswich) have reinforced the picture provided in the documentary sources. At Hamwic, the town's inhabitants were busy smithing bronze and iron, and working with gold and lead. Boneworking was an important activity, as was pottery making, textile production and leather- and woodworking. The town had a mint, and coins circulated freely in the town. Shoppers in Hamwic could also purchase exotic goods newly imported from the Continent. Finds from the site include pottery from Belgium, Germany and France, quernstones from the Eifel Mountains in Germany, whetstones from Normandy, and glass vessels from the Rhineland.

In addition to the permanent centres of trade – the wic sites – there were also a number of temporary, seasonal markets or fairs. Evidence for these sites has been provided by recent metal-detector finds, which are beginning to show concentrations of activity at sites where previously no settlements have been found or recorded in the documentary evidence. It is not yet clear how these 'productive sites' worked, but an excavation of a riverside site near Eton may give some insights. Here, no permanent settlement was found, but there was evidence for rubbish pits, which had been dug over successive seasons, for smithing, and for trading. Finds included high-status Tating-ware – a black pottery with silver inlay from Germany – which indicates that these fairs were more than local. It is possible that Continental traders made seasonal journeys up the River Thames to similar temporary markets.

Early Anglo-Saxon style is visible in the excavated costumes of the dead. The traditional burial dress of Anglo-Saxon women was regional, and derived from their Germanic homelands. The standard dress consisted of a tube-shaped *peplos* garment, secured at the shoulders with a pair of brooches, worn over a long-sleeved undergarment, with a cloak, cape or shawl over the top, which in turn might be fastened by a third brooch. Long strings of beads might be suspended from the paired brooches. The size, shape, decoration and composition of the brooches indicated status, regional affiliations and wealth. The simplest were cast from iron: the most ostentatious were made with gold, garnet and other precious or semi-precious materials. A belt was worn at the waist, which also offered the opportunity to suspend further decorative items from it, including pouches, keys, decorative metalwork and further strings of beads.

Mineralised textile adhering to the underside of a brooch worn as part of a mortuary costume.

The Soay is the ancestor of all modern sheep breeds. They are small, shed their short brown fleeces, and are naturally short-tailed.

Costumes were colourful. Sheep in Anglo-Saxon England were small and dark brown, or there were white sheep introduced by the Romans, and wool came in a range of natural colours. Surviving fragments of cloth show that textiles were woven with herringbone or tartan patterns, and natural dyes allowed clothes to be coloured red, blue, green, orange and yellow. Edges would be finished with a tablet-woven braid – surviving examples show that these braids, too, would have complicated, colourful patterns. Examples from Barking Abbey and the cloak of the man buried at Taplow included gold thread. Even shoes might have decorative buckles. The strings of beads, too, were polychrome, with beads made of different coloured glass, amber, crystal, and jet.

In Kent, some women wore an additional garment which came into fashion in the sixth century, copying Continental Frankish fashion. This consisted of a front-opening coat fastened with two brooches that went over the *peplos* gown: some high-status Kentish women were therefore buried with two pairs of brooches.

Wool dyed in colours derived from weld (green and yellow), woad (blue) and madder (red).

In an era when few people would have had access to many sets of clothing, it is likely that, certainly at the lower end of the social scale, people would have worn the same costume every day – their clothes were part of their identity. This may explain, perhaps, the readiness of Anglo-Saxons to place so many clothing goods in the grave with the dead, for the brooches worn by the dead were personal and intimately associated with them.

Example of Anglo-Saxon weaving on a vertical loom at West Stow Anglo-Saxon village.

With the introduction of Christianity, costumes for women changed, taking inspiration from Byzantium. The long chains of beads were replaced by smaller necklaces. Amber, so important in earlier bead strings, became rare, and instead silver and gold beads and linked rings became more fashionable. The traditional pairs of brooches with their zoomorphic interlace were replaced, if at all, by a single round composite brooch, decorated with gold, garnet and shell inlay. Headdresses also become more common in this period. Delicate linked pins found by women's heads indicate that veils made of fine linen, or even silk in the case of elite women, were being worn.

Men, it appears, dressed as brightly as women. They may not have had pairs of brooches or beads, but they did have buckles – the bigger, the better. In addition to being a practical way of securing the belt from which pouches, swords, knives and other masculine paraphernalia were hung, belts may have served to indicate rank, a practice derived from Roman military costume. One of the earliest datable Anglo-Saxon burials is that of a man interred in Dyke Hills, just outside Dorchester-on-Thames, in Oxfordshire. Dorchester was a Roman town, which seems to have persisted as a settlement into the fifth century. The man buried at Dyke Hills had a Roman-style military belt with fittings decorated in a chip-carved style typical of the fourth century, but burial with grave goods was not a Romano-British practice. In the early seventh century, the man at Sutton Hoo was also buried with a stunning belt buckle. It was made of gold, and was over thirteen centimetres long. It was skilfully decorated with

A decorated sword hilt from a seventh-century male grave at Finglesham, Kent. The ring fixed to the pommel denoted status.

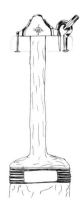

Elite male warrior or ceremonial costume.

interlaced biting animals. It was, however, an imitation buckle, which had to be sewn onto the costume – the buckle was symbolic, rather than functional, suggesting that the wearing of a large buckle was a sign of status in elite male costume, for both the living and the dead. Men wore short, belted tunics and close-fitting trousers. By the seventh century, elite men were also wearing long cloaks, like the yellow-dyed cloak placed with the man buried at Mound 1, Sutton Hoo.

For both men and women, status was indicated not so much in the style of clothing, as in the material used – wool, linen or silk – and in the quality and cost of the decorative items added to the costume, such as brooches, belts and embroideries. Ecclesiastical men wore mass vestments – long, loose clothes covering their legs: along with their tonsures, their clothes would have marked out their difference from men in secular society. Religious women's dress was probably an undecorated version of the secular dress of women: in her later life, St Hilda regretted the bright beads she had worn before she joined the church.

A field of flax. Flax was the source of linen for elite clothes: breaking down the plant fibres to make yarn consumed considerable time and energy.

Surviving cloth from graves shows very little sign of felting, suggesting that clothing was rarely, if ever, washed. For woollen clothing, this would have had the advantage of maintaining the natural waterproofing of the material.

Hairstyles were a matter of importance in Anglo-Saxon society, and indicated age and status. This may explain the ferocity of the debate in the new Anglo-Saxon church about the use of the Celtic tonsure, at the front of the hairline, or the new Roman tonsure, at the top of the head, which became a matter of heated confrontation in the mid-seventh century. Secular men are rarely depicted wearing head coverings unless they were wearing helmets for battle, and even the helmet from Sutton Hoo, which covered the face, features an imitation moustache, suggesting that facial hair carried important symbolic messages for elite men. Few images of men or women survive from this period, but male faces on button brooches, for example, show short hair brushed stiffly back from the forehead, and carefully trimmed moustaches, with cheeks bare.

A gilt bronze button brooch from Buckland, Kent.

The burial evidence indicates that children wore much simpler versions of the adult dress. Their clothes-fasteners were probably wooden toggles, since few brooches or buckles are found in children's graves. It may be that children wore very little, especially in the warmer months. In the Old English version of St Cuthbert's life, it is recorded that, when he was a little boy, Cuthbert and his friends played boisterous games with no clothes on – a detail removed in the Latin version of the Life.

The church had a profound influence on Anglo-Saxon style. The influence started at the top of the social hierarchy. Kings wished to impose their rule and assert their right to kingship, and one of the ways they did this was by emulating Continental fashions and ideals. Aristocrats followed suit. The very decorative and visually arresting gold and garnet jewellery of the seventh century is an expression of this intention. Whereas, in the fifth and sixth centuries, costumes – especially women's costumes – showed regional affiliations, by the seventh century, gold and garnet jewellery, often decorated with a cruciform motif, was used by the elite to separate themselves from the rest of the population. Gold and garnet pendants are found, for example, in Kent, Suffolk, Norfolk and Gloucestershire.

Merchants and locals go about their business on the waterfront in seventh-century Hamwic. Boats, many coated with pitch to waterproof them, are pulled up on the shore. Goods are being unloaded, loaded and traded. The rich clothes of visiting merchants shine out against the more earthy tones worn by poorer locals. Along the patchy gravelled road, the houses display a variety of building and roofing styles. (Artwork by Dominic Andrews)

TRANSPORT

THE PRIMARY METHOD of transport for all Anglo-Saxons was by foot, and, for most people, journeys would have been local. Longer journeys, away from the neighbourhood, would have been more difficult, not just because there were few good paths, but also because there were social restrictions on the movement of people across the landscape. Wihtred of Kent (d. 725) decreed that a servant travelling on his own on Sundays was to pay his lord compensation. Independent travel for most people was effectively against the law: travel should only be on the lord's business.

Some land routes across the country did exist, largely consisting of an inherited network of pathways including ancient routes such as the Ridgeway paths, and Roman roads. Distributions of Anglo-Saxon settlements indicate the extent to which it was helpful for settlements to be located within easy walking distance of the old roads – close enough to access them for travel and trade, but not so close that the settlement would offer an easily visible target for passing gangs. Travellers were the elite, traders with royal or local authority to travel, people travelling with the authorisation of their masters, and later, churchmen and pilgrims. Some churchmen, like kings with their households, travelled in large groups. Abbot Ceolfrith of Monkwearmouth-Jarrow, for example, travelled with eighty foot companions – a serious challenge in terms of food supply and expense: he died in Burgundy in AD 716 en route to Rome.

Horses would have provided transport for the elite. At Sutton Hoo and at Lakenheath, Suffolk, for example, horses with richly decorated trappings were buried in graves next to young males. There appear to have been some taboos associated with

Opposite: Part of the Ridgeway in Oxfordshire.

Below: Elite males used horses, ornamented with decorated harness, to express their high status. Horses may also have had a cultic significance.

A reconstruction
of an Anglo-Saxon
ship.

the riding of horses. Horse bridal fittings and trappings, and horse burials, are almost exclusively associated with male burials, suggesting that horse riding was an aspect of male, rather than female, elite identity (though it does not necessarily mean that women never rode horses). Bede recounts that in AD 627 when Coifi, formerly a pagan priest of the temple at Goodmanham in Northumbria, converted to Christianity, he climbed on a stallion, which broke pagan sacred law, and threw a spear into the shrine of the pagan gods he had worshipped. When the young St Wilfred (AD 634–709) arrived at a monastery on horseback, hoping to become a monk, the monks thought he was a warrior and would not let him in. Hengist and Horsa, the legendary first Anglo-Saxon invaders of England, have names that mean 'horse' and 'mare', which may hint at early pagan worship of horses. Early Anglo-Saxon women's cruciform brooches had a developed version of a horse's head making up the lower bar of the brooch, again suggesting that the image of the horse had ritual or occult meaning.

Port Meadow,
Oxford – the
Thames was
already channelled
to aid navigation
at Oxford in the
eighth century.

With the development of wics and kingdoms, it was essential for the maintenance of royal power and for the economy that routes were kept open, roads repaired, and bridges rebuilt. Early law codes show the extent to which this was a priority for rulers: road and bridge taxes were levied on the population. But the sea and rivers were also essential for trade and travel in early Anglo-Saxon England. The importance of the rivers is exemplified by the distribution of types of metalwork in Buckinghamshire. Artefacts suggest that the north of the county was in close contact with Northamptonshire, making use of the Great Ouse, and the people in the east of the county were linked, through the Thames Valley, with Bedfordshire, Hertfordshire and London.

Very few Anglo-Saxon boats have survived from this period. The most well known is the ship from the Mound 1 burial at Sutton Hoo. Only the iron rivets survived from this boat, but the 1939 excavators of the site were so professional that they were able to pick out the impression of the decayed timbers in the sands of the barrow. The original boat was clinker-built and was around 27 metres long. It had rowlocks, indicating that at least some of its power came from rowers. A much simpler log boat, measuring 3 metres in length, was used as a coffin at the nearby early Anglo-Saxon cemetery of Snape.

There is still a debate about whether boats like the one at Sutton Hoo would have had sails. The Sutton Hoo ship was a sea-going vessel, and experimental reconstructions of the boat show that, even though it did not have a deep keel, it could have taken a sail. There is evidence that rivers were maintained for navigation purposes, just as roads were. Excavations by the Thames, for example, have shown channels to control the river dating to the eighth century at Oxford, and a mid-Saxon channel marker has been found in Holy Brook at Coley Park Farm, in Berkshire. Roads and waterways were linked. In Kent, land routes connected directly to important harbours. In a grant by Frithuwold, sub-king of Surrey, to Chertsey in AD 672/674, ships were described as coming in to harbour at the port of London 'by the public road'.

Above: Travel was dependent on seasons and the weather.

Taplow burial mound. Like Sutton Hoo, the burial at Taplow commands a view of the river – in this case the Thames.

51

RELAXATION AND ENTERTAINMENT

MUCH OF THE ENTERTAINMENT in early Anglo-Saxon England focused on the hall. Feasting provided some of the fun, but the mealtime was also an opportunity for storytelling, as the many Old English poems which were later written down indicate. There might be a professional storyteller (*scop*) in the hall, or those present might take their turn at recounting tales. Stories of the heroic deeds of old were the most popular, even in Christian times, as the complaints of clerics show. One solution was to present the Christian story as a heroic tale. A good example of this is the poem known as *The Dream of the Rood*. In its earliest form, the opening lines of it are cut in runic script on a stone cross at Ruthwell. In the poem, Christ is portrayed as a typical secular warrior, showing no fear and commanding the loyalty of his men.

Music might accompany the storytelling. Although there may have been paid musicians, every one, from the king down, was supposed to be able to provide a turn. One of the earliest conversion stories explains that the cowherd Caedmon, who worked in the monastery of St Hilda, was too ashamed of his poor singing skills to take his turn when it came to the entertainments, and went to hide in the cowshed and pray. Miraculously, his prayers were answered, and he was able to return to the hall to sing a sweet song in praise of God.

One form of Anglo-Saxon communal entertainment involved wordplay. Some riddles provided intellectual challenges, but many were intentionally ribald: highly suggestive riddles survive for which correct, though not immediately obvious, answers were 'dough', 'cock and hen', 'poker' and 'key'.

Some musical instruments survive. Illustrations suggest that there were horns and tambourines, and in the Vespasian Psalter, there is an illustration of the biblical King David playing the lyre. A similar instrument was found in the royal tomb of the man – perhaps King Redwald – buried in Mound 1 at Sutton Hoo, Suffolk. A lyre was also

Opposite: In this page from the early eighth-century Vespasian Psalter, produced in southern England, King David is shown playing the lyre surrounded by his scribes and musicians.

Above: Feasting in the hall – an opportunity to exchange news and teach politics to children.

Below: Tales of heroic battle are the mainstay of surviving secular poetry.

found interred with the high-status male at Taplow, Buckinghamshire, but discoveries of lyres interred with bodies at early Anglo-Saxon inhumation sites such as Bergh Apton, Norfolk and Saxton Road, Abingdon, Oxfordshire indicate that men of lower status could also own such instruments. So far, all known lyres are from male graves.

The elite played board games, though only playing pieces, not the boards, have survived. Several excavated aristocratic burials – at Mound 1, Sutton Hoo, at Taplow, Buckinghamshire, and at Prittlewell, Essex, had gaming pieces amongst all the other finery in the graves. The man at Prittlewell, and the aristocrat buried at Asthall Barrow, Oxfordshire, were also equipped with dice. Few gaming pieces survive from lower-status settlements, but finds of bone dice suggest that gambling also provided a source of amusement. Hunting with dogs and birds of prey probably formed part of the aristocratic lifestyle. Occasionally, dogs have been found buried within cemetery sites – two dog graves were excavated at Great Chesterford, Essex.

When men and women were not working, ritual and religion occupied a significant proportion of the day. The festivals of the Christian calendar reflect many of the ritual feasts and celebrations of the pagan past, in their seasonality and perhaps also in some of their activities. Evidence for pagan belief and practice is, however, limited. The Christian writers who offered the first proper written evidence for the period, for example, were not interested in explaining earlier pagan beliefs or belief systems, only in getting rid of them – illustrated by the decision taken at the Synod of Clofesho in AD 747 to ban 'divines, soothsayers, auguries, auspices, amulets, enchantments or any other filth of the ungodly' – or in adapting and re-using pagan places to bring them into the church, a policy famously promoted by Pope Gregory the Great.

Our best evidence for the names of pagan deities comes from our most everyday modern nouns – the days of the week. Tuesday recalls the god Tiw; Wednesday recalls Woden, Thursday recalls Thunor, and Friday recalls Frey/Freya/Frig. A few other gods are known from other modern words; Easter, the most important Christian festival, is named after the goddess Eostra, who presumably had an important festival at this time of the year in the early Anglo-Saxon world. She was so important that her name survives to this day, but we know absolutely nothing else for certain about her, or about how her festival was organised.

Counters for a board game were placed at the head of the body buried in the ship at Mound 1, Sutton Hoo, as illustrated in this reconstruction.

Place names give some more useful evidence about early Anglo-Saxon paganism. Sacred places survive in the landscape: places with an 'eccles' (from the Latin *ecclesia*, meaning 'church') component marked pre-Anglo-Saxon churches, such as Eccles (Kent) and Beccles (Suffolk), founded by the Christianised Romano-British. On the other hand, place names containing the element *hearg* (Harrow, Harrowden), or *weoh, wih* (Weedon, Weoley, Willey), suggest the location of a heathen shrine. There are also a number of place names in the landscape that are associated with Old English gods or other supernatural beings: the gods Tiw, Woden and Thunor are commemorated in place names such as Tysoe, Wednesbury and Thursley.

Some place names contain the element *Grim*, meaning 'the masked one', a nickname for Woden. This element is particularly associated with the prehistoric ditches and other earthworks crossing the English landscape: Grims Ditch, Grimsdyke, Grimsbury (Oxfordshire) and Grimes Graves (Norfolk). Lesser deities are also present in the landscape: goblins (*puca* and *hob*) are both attested in place names, and there are documentary references to the *feldelve* – field elf.

A typical early medieval bone die.

There are hints that burial grounds were places where some ritual activity took place. Mounds and posts were placed over some graves, suggesting that there was a wish to remember or commemorate the dead. Some burial grounds include small structures, such as the little four-post building erected over cremations in Alton, Hampshire;

Above: The eighth-century Ruthwell Cross, Dumfriesshire, is decorated with Biblical scenes and plant and animal ornament, and has inscriptions in Latin and runic script. The runes preserve part of the poem *The Dream of the Rood.*

Lechlade, Gloucestershire; Berinsfield, Oxfordshire; and Apple Down, Hampshire.

Amongst the burials within Anglo-Saxon cemeteries were a number of animals whose bodies were unlikely to be food offerings, particularly dogs and horses. Their presence in graves may be related to statements about the wealth and power of the dead, but they may also have had other ritual associations. Animals were conspicuous in early Anglo-Saxon art. A number of surviving Anglo-Saxon myths and illustrations suggest that some animals were thought to be sacred or to have ritual significance. The boar had a special place in Anglo-Saxon folklore, being particularly associated with battle: a boar figure decorates the crest of the helmet found buried with a sixth-century Mercian warrior at Benty Grange, Derbyshire, for example. According to surviving myth, the boar was sacred to the Vanir, Germanic fertility gods.

Beowulf, the hero of the Old English poem, was unusual for an aristocrat, because he had a name that did not alliterate with any other names in his family. His name may have been a nickname: Beowulf means 'bear', and Beowulf is characterised by the extraordinary physical strength that enabled him to fight the monster Grendel with his bare hands. 'Wulf', by contrast, was a common element in male and female names (Wulfwaru, Wulfric, Aethelwulf), and '*heorot*', 'stag', also occurs in names (Heorogar), and was the name given to Hrothgar's royal hall, which Grendel attempted to destroy. An illustration of the palace of King David in the Continental Utrecht Psalter shows a stag's head crowning the gable, and the stag figure surmounting the whetstone at Sutton Hoo suggests that the symbolic association between the stag and kingship was established by the seventh century in England.

Birds had a special place in Anglo-Saxon ritual. They occur as beaked heads in early Anglo-Saxon metalwork, or as bird-shaped brooches, imported from the Continent. Eagles and ravens had particular resonance within heroic warrior mythology: birds could

Right: Writhing interlaced dragons – visual puzzles – were a common motif in early Anglo-Saxon art.

move between this world ('middle earth') and the worlds above and below. Images of biting birds occur in particular association with images of warriors: the Sutton Hoo helmet, for example, has images of dancing warriors on the helmet plates, who are themselves wearing helmets adorned with beaked heads. An early-seventh-century gilt bronze buckle found in a grave at Finglesham, Kent, depicts a man carrying two spears. He is naked except for a buckled belt and a helmet topped by two opposing bird heads.

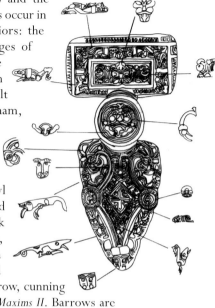

The dragon is everywhere in early Anglo-Saxon art. Snake-like dragons writhe and crawl across Anglo-Saxon metalwork in complicated woven patterns, from the finest gold metalwork found in the richest graves to simple, inexpensive disc brooches worn in daily life. In the literary sources, dragons are associated with treasure: 'the dragon belongs in its barrow, cunning and jealous of its jewels' wrote the poet of *Maxims II*. Barrows are burial mounds: the dragon was the symbolic guardian of the world's hidden treasures.

Domestic buildings may also have served as special or hallowed spaces. When St Augustine came to England, King Aethelbert of Kent insisted that the meeting with the newcomer should take place in the open air. The practical reason for this was probably that he wanted all his followers to be able to witness the meeting, but the reason Bede gave was that Aethelbert held to the superstition that magic traps could have been laid for him if he had held the meeting in a building.

Other evidence hints at everyday superstitions and rituals. The *Beowulf* poet referred to the ancient art of sortilege, and a collection of animal astragali bones found in a later-fifth-century cremation urn at Casitor-by-Norwich, Norfolk, might have been intended for use in foretelling the future by 'reading' the pattern of bones thrown on the ground. The collection of bones at Caistor-by-Norwich has only drawn attention because of its unusual context, but other household items may have been put to occult purposes.

Above: Brooch with a complex interplay of entwining mythical beasts in its decoration.

Below: Runic writing on the pommel of a sword from Gilton, Kent – the runes are indecipherable.

EDUCATION AND SOCIAL SERVICE

OBJECTS that we can recognise as children's toys are almost entirely absent from the archaeological record. There are no certain finds of, for example, dolls, miniature toys, or any other play equipment. When children died and were buried, they were interred with a few adult items, but not with any items only associated with children. Children will play with whatever comes to hand, however, and many of the broken and worn objects found in settlement excavations may have passed through children's hands as 'toys' before entering the archaeological record. Other 'toys', mentioned in later Old English sources, such as sticks (play swords and hobby-horses) and reeds (play boats) will not survive in the archaeological record.

Some evidence of the training boys were given is evident from their grave goods. Weapons – swords, spears, shields and arrows – were the markers of high-status adult males. Some boys, however, were also buried with weapons. Spearheads appear in the graves of some children from the age of about five. There is a direct correlation between the average length of the spearhead and the age of the person with which it is found, and this holds true right through the lifecycle. It is reasonable to suggest that children were given spearheads of an appropriate size for their age partly to show their immaturity, but also, perhaps, because these were the spearheads the boys were supposed to begin practising and training with. The age of legal responsibility, according to the earliest law codes, was as young as ten – this was the age at which an orphaned child could take charge of his inheritance, swear oaths of loyalty to his lord, and take his place as an adult in society. It is not unlikely, then, that boys would start training for their coming role as adults from about six or seven.

It is much less clear what training girls received, though learning to make textiles was probably among their tasks. Grave goods associated with girls show that, from about the age of twelve, more adult-related objects would be placed with girls, and, as for boys, this age marks the

Opposite:
Sandbach Cross:
reconstruction
of an open-air
service. Anglo-
Saxon sculpture
was often brightly
painted.

Age and spearhead length from the cemetery of Great Chesterford, Essex. Spearhead length is a marker of age and status.

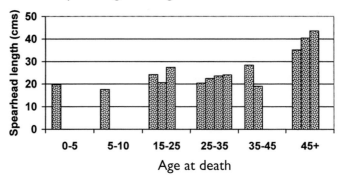

Spear length and age at Great Chesterford

A mid-seventh to mid-eighth-century grave marker from Lindisfarne, commemorating a female named Osgyth. Her name is written in both runes and Anglo-Saxon capitals.

Spindle whorls from the excavated settlement at West Stow. Whorls were used to spin yarn, and were made of a variety of materials, including re-used Roman pot bases. Girls would have learnt the techniques of spinning from an early age.

beginning of adult-related tasks and responsibilities, though the full repertoire of female grave goods is only found in the graves of women who died in their early twenties or later. Early law codes indicate, though, that there were social and legal limits to the age at which a girl was considered old enough for marriage: a law code on the rape of an 'underage' girl indicates as much.

It is probable that some of the 'training' given to children involved taking responsibility for tasks in the home and in the fields. The young St Cuthbert tended sheep when he was a child. Higher-status boys had other training. The eighth-century *Life* of St Guthlac illustrates the kind of education available to aristocratic boys at this time. Although both Guthlac's parents were Christian and noble, he was not taught to read or write. Instead, his biographer complained that he only learned by listening to poetry in the halls, which inspired him to leave home when he reached adolescence and ride out as the leader of a war band.

The songs in the halls were not idle entertainment. Later documentary sources praised men who were *leothcræftig* (skilled in song) and able to give *leothorun* (wise counsel in song). One surviving Old English poem, *Widsith*, gives an insight into the functions of the poetry sung in the hall: in a time before written records were common, poetry stored a communal hoard of important memories about the origins of feuds, land rights, boundaries, obligations through marriage, dynastic history and important political news.

An example of
a lucet cord
worked on a
sheep metatarsal.

Surviving musical
instruments are
associated with
male burials, but
later Anglo-Saxon
documents
indicate that
women, too,
could be
entertainers.

With the introduction of Christianity, learning to read and write in Latin as well as English became part of the education of some girls and boys who were given to the church from an early age – oblates like Bede, who was taken to Monkwearmouth-Jarrow and given to

Literacy extended beyond the church: this runic writing on the back of a mended brooch from Harford Farm, Norfolk reads 'L/Tuda mended this brooch'.

Benedict Biscop when he was seven. The first English school was established at Canterbury by Augustine and his missionaries shortly after their arrival in England in AD 597, and the success of this school is attested by the fact that native Anglo-Saxons trained at Canterbury were able to supply the teachers at a new school founded by Sigeberht, King of East Anglia, in the 630s.

Bede's writings reflect his education – he was taught grammar, Bible studies, chanting and *computus* (computation of time, specifically the calculation of the date of Easter in the Christian calendar), and Latin. Girls who were destined for the ecclesiastical life were also taught to a high level of literacy. Some correspondence between five Anglo-Saxon women and the Anglo-Saxon missionary Boniface has survived, including letters from Leofgyth (d. AD 771), who was taught by Abbess Eadburg at Minster, and then by Abbess Tetta at Wimborne. Leofgyth's first surviving letter to Boniface was written while she was still relatively young, and in it she asks Boniface to pray for her parents; and she also invited him to correct any mistakes in her Latin. Later, Leofgyth became the abbess of Tauberbischofsheim in Germany, and her own writings influenced the work of other monks and nuns.

Law codes indicate that aspects of what we would now call 'social services' – care of the young, the elderly, the poor and the sick – were effectively in the hands of the family and neighbouring community. With the introduction of Christianity, the church also took on a role of caring for the socially vulnerable. Bede's description of St Hilda's famous double monastery at Whitby in the seventh century included a building where the sick and terminally ill were looked after; and Bede further records a number of monks and nuns who were victims of paralysis or extremely debilitating illness who were nonetheless cared for and kept alive for considerable periods of time, including Torhtgyth, a nun who had been severely ill for nine years, and another 'certain nun, of noble family' who had been 'so disabled that she could not move a single limb' for many years.

Demones arcüdü
domū Guchī ⁊ diuer
sis formis bestiaⁿ

Guthlacus

HEALTH

Early Anglo-Saxon health can only be teased out on the basis of the skeletal evidence. Unfortunately, with very rare exceptions (the mummified body of St Cuthbert being one), only bones survive, and then not necessarily in good condition. Knowledge of the period is also hampered because it seems probable that not everyone was buried in the community cemetery. There are not enough infant burials in most early cemeteries, for example, suggesting that dead infants, at least, might more normally be buried elsewhere. A number of infant bones have been found in association with settlements such as West Stow, Suffolk, West Heslerton, Yorkshire, and Barrow Hills, Oxfordshire.

At Berinsfield, Oxfordshire, more than half the females represented by the buried population had died by the age of thirty. Males at this site did rather better, as only eight of the twenty-six had died before the age of thirty. On average, only 10 per cent of the population represented by the skeletons found in early Anglo-Saxon populations survived to live for more than forty-five years, without taking into account the many infants and younger children not buried in the community cemeteries.

Estimates of stature based on the skeletal evidence from cemeteries offer a surprisingly consistent story across Anglo-Saxon England. The earliest cemeteries, from the fifth to the sixth centuries, show that the population buried in these Germanic burial grounds was a little taller than the population associated with the late Romano-British cemeteries, with males standing at about 173 cm and females at around 162 cm on average.

There may (controversially) be a genetic dimension to the increase in height in the earlier Anglo-Saxon population compared to the native British population, but height is also related to diet. The evidence from the early Anglo-Saxon inhumation cemeteries shows that the population was relatively healthy, with little bone evidence for diseases caused by malnutrition or deficiency in the diet. Skeletal evidence and stable isotope analysis also shows that there was no significant difference in diet between men and women, although there is some

Opposite:
In this illustration from the medieval *Life* of St Guthlac produced in England, St Guthlac drives out a devil from a mad man.

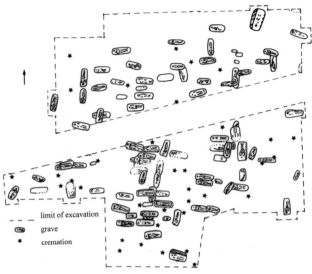

evidence from the little stable isotope analysis that has been done to suggest that, at the site of Berinsfield in Oxfordshire, at least, young adult males enjoyed a diet rich in the best proteins – sheep and cattle – while older males ate more fish and pork.

Because only skeletal evidence is available for study, only diseases and traumas which were severe enough to have an impact on the bones can be identified. It is rarely possible to say caused a person's death.

Plan of an early Anglo-Saxon mixed-rite cemetery at Worthy Park, Kings Worthy, Hampshire. Inhumation cemeteries are the best source of information for early Anglo-Saxon health.

The skeletons that have been excavated – and they now number in the thousands – are characterised by having remarkably little evidence of malnutrition and trauma compared to earlier and later groups. Wear and tear on the joints characterises most adult skeletons in the cemetery record. Almost all Anglo-Saxon adults had back problems from vertebral degeneration, probably as a result of the wear and tear of daily life. Men seemed to suffer from back trouble at an earlier age than women, perhaps related to their heavier work. Osteoarthritis in joints is also visible in a significant number of Anglo-Saxon skeletons, with hips the most common joint to suffer, but cases of osteoarthritis at wrists, elbows, knees, ankles and shoulders are also prevalent.

Weapon injury is rare. The documentary sources give the impression that the early Anglo-Saxon settlers in England were warlike and engaged in constant battles with their neighbours, and the emphasis in the male adult burial ritual on weaponry reinforces the impression of a military society. But the skeletons offer a different story. It may be that much of the fighting was carried out between the elite. Gift exchange, negotiation, hostage taking, feasting and marriage agreements would all have been important stages before hostilities were engaged in, and, judging from the ostentatious gold and garnet decoration on the sword pommels, shields and other weaponry associated with the elite seventh-century burials, bravado and posturing were also key aspects of any disagreements between rival tribes or kingdoms. Battles, when they occurred, were undoubtedly exciting and memorable events which might have a significant impact on the political future of a kingdom, but interpersonal violence at the local level seems to have been rare.

At Berinsfield, Oxfordshire, no one had lost teeth through dental decay before the age of thirty, and caries was rare – this pattern is replicated in other Anglo-Saxon cemetery sites. When teeth did

Early Anglo-Saxon personal hygiene – ear-scoops and tweezers from West Stow.

become infected, however, there was little remedy for the pain. One skeleton at Berinsfield had defective enamel on the molars, which led to a number of untreated caries, which would have caused the individual to suffer from constant discomfort and debilitating low-level infection. Another individual from the same site had a large carious cavity on one side of the jaw. The teeth on the affected side were noticeably less worn than on the healthy side, showing the care the sufferer had taken not to chew on the painful side.

Several cases of tuberculosis and leprosy are recorded for the Anglo-Saxon period. Assessment of the treatment of those identified with leprosy (or a similarly disfiguring, chronic disease) in the early Anglo-Saxon period suggests that they were given special rituals at death, which may be because their illness gave them special status. At Edix Hill, Cambridgeshire, for example, three cases of women with disfiguring tubercular diseases are also amongst the very richest in the cemetery. At Beckford, two burials identified as being leprous were buried slightly away from the main cemetery (though the site was only partially excavated), and both, again, were given rich grave goods.

A weapon wound to a skull from Buckland. The victim probably did not die from the injury since the wound shows signs of healing.

Though invisible in the archaeological evidence, the documentary sources report outbreaks of 'plague' devastating parts of the country. Bede records that one outbreak in AD 664 depopulated southern Britain first, before moving northwards and then into Ireland. Bede names various monks who were killed by the plague, but he also offers cases of survivors. An Anglo-Saxon monk called Egbert, living in Ireland, caught the plague of AD 664, but recovered and lived to be ninety, dying in AD 729.

There is not much evidence for Anglo-Saxon cleanliness and personal hygiene.

Early Anglo-Saxon mortuary costume sometimes included small metal items hanging from belts, which have been interpreted as ear-scoops and tweezers. They are found with adults of all ages, but are relatively more common in the graves of older people. Perhaps water was too valuable a commodity to waste on washing, because in the eighth century Benedict Biscop sent Boniface a gift of a bath towel, a face towel and a little frankincense (*'sabanum unum et facitergium unem et modica thymiana'*), but it may be that the cloth in this gift was of particularly high quality, and the inclusion of frankincense in the gift implies that the items were intended to be used in a ritual or specialised way. Evidence for head lice still caught in the teeth of abandoned bone combs from ninth-century Coppergate tells an evocative tale of everyday discomfort due to lice infestations.

The surviving evidence suggests that Anglo-Saxon sanitation was rudimentary. Examples of latrine pits are rare in early and rural Anglo-Saxon settlement contexts. At West Stow, Suffolk, for example, three abandoned sunken-featured buildings contained cess, though it was impossible to be certain whether the material was of human or animal origin. If it was human, it means that people were defecating in limited and selected areas. It is probable that much human waste was collected for manuring the fields. The word used to describe a toilet was the same as that used for a manure heap: the Old English word *feltun* meant both 'privy' and 'dunghill'.

Evidence for early medicine is also scant. Beads worn by women, especially amber and crystal beads, may have been thought to ward off evil, as were, perhaps, the animal teeth and fossils carried in pouches. The serpentine animals, boars, horses, birds of prey and human faces which appeared on pre-Christian jewellery may also have been protective charms, to be replaced by crosses and fish motifs with the introduction of Christianity. With the arrival of Christianity, the church took on a role in the healing process. Bede cites a doctor named Cynefrith, who attended the saintly Queen Aethelthryth before her death, and who was present at her body's exhumation from the grave and translation into a church in a new coffin some sixteen years later. Cynefrith stated that he had lanced a tumour on the Queen's jaw before her death, but that when her body was dug up to move it to its new grave, the gaping wound had miraculously healed. The best-recorded Anglo-Saxon church

Decorated cremation urn from West Stow – the decorations stamped on the pot may have had cultic or amuletic significance.

Binsey Well, Oxford. Associated with St Frideswide, the water is reputed to have healing powers.

doctor was Bishop John of Beverley, who died in AD 721. Visiting an abbess, he was informed that her daughter was fatally ill with a swollen arm, and was asked to make her better. Asking the circumstances of her illness (asking for a history, as any modern family doctor would before attempting a diagnosis), John discovered that the girl had been bled, to which he retorted that that it had been a foolish and ignorant action to bleed her on the fourth day of the moon, and he recalled that Archbishop Theodore had taught him that it was dangerous to bleed a patient when the moon was waxing and the tide flowing.

Archbishop Theodore was sent to England in AD 668 by Pope Vitalian. Theodore was a native of Tarsus in Cilicia, and was described by Bede as 'well trained in secular and divine literature, both Greek and Latin'. It was through foreign church scholars that Greek and Latin literature, including medical literature, was first brought to the Anglo-Saxons, and Bishop John was a product of their training. John's miracles, as recorded by Bede, illustrate that the Greek and Roman medical tradition was alive and working in seventh-century Anglo-Saxon England, and that it was a first course of action in the case of illness. Only when it was clear that 'conventional' medicine would fail, was John credited with miraculous healing.

The church would also have acted as a focus for prayer and belief in miraculous cures. The scrap of silk found in a metal container placed in the late sixth-/early seventh-century grave of a baby from Updown, Kent, may have been an amuletic relic taken from silks imported for ecclesiastical vestments in the early days of Christianity.

From the first appearance of Anglo-Saxon culture in England to England on the eve of the arrival of the Vikings, society, religion, culture, fashion, language, work and education had changed dramatically. With the arrival of the Vikings, the Anglo-Saxons would have to adapt again.

Christian imagery on a seventh-century belt buckle from Eccles, Kent, perhaps intended to give divine protection to the wearer.

PLACES TO VISIT

Bede's World, Church Bank, Jarrow NE32 3DY. Tel. 01914 892106.

   Built to represent the life of Bede, the centre includes a museum,
   a reconstructed early Anglo-Saxon farm and monastic workshop.
   St Paul's church, where Bede would have worshipped, can be visited.

Bewcastle Cross, Bewcastle Church, Cumbria, CA6 6DA.

   The seventh-century cross is still in its original position in the churchyard.

The Priory Church, Breedon on the Hill, Leicestershire DE73 8AJ.

   An Anglo-Saxon monastery was established within an Iron Age hillfort
   here in AD 676.

Bradwell on Sea, Essex CM0 7PX.

   The chapel of St Peter-on-the-wall was built into the Roman fort in the
   seventh century. One of the earliest Anglo-Saxon churches in the country.

British Museum, Great Russell Street, London WC1B 3DG. Tel. 0207 3238299.

   The 'Europe AD 300–1100' gallery includes displays of the original
   artefacts from the Mound 1 ship burial at Sutton Hoo.

Burgh Castle, near Great Yarmouth, Norfolk.

   Built in the late third or fourth century as part of the network of
   Roman Saxon Shore forts, the surviving three walls of the fort are an
   impressive sight. The seventh-century St Fursey may have established a
   church within the walls.

Corinium Museum, Park Street, Cirencester GL7 2BX. Tel. 01285 655611.

   The museum exhibits include finds from the nationally important
   Butler's Field cemetery, Lechlade.

Durham Cathedral, The College, Durham DH1 3EH. Tel. 01913 864266.

   The imposing Norman cathedral was built around the shrine of
   St Cuthbert. Cuthbert's relics are on display and the cathedral also
   houses the head of St Oswald and the remains of the Venerable Bede.

Dyke Hills, Dorchester-on-Thames, Oxfordshire.

   Very early Anglo-Saxon burials – possibly representing the earliest
   Germanic mercenaries and their families – dug into the Iron Age
   ramparts which lie just outside the Roman town of Dorchester.

Escomb Church, Bishop Auckland, County Durham.

   Church built before the end of the seventh century.

Offa's Dyke, Knighton, Powys LD7 1EN.

   The eighth-century earthwork built by King Offa of Mercia runs from
   Prestatyn in the North to Chepstow in the South.

Lindisfarne, Northumberland TD15 2SE.

   St Aidan founded his monastery on Lindisfarne in AD 635: also home to
   St Cuthbert, the monastery was of international importance. As well as
   the remains of the later medieval monastery, the Island has a museum
   and an exhibition centre with facsimiles of the *Lindisfarne Gospels*.

Ruthwell, Dumfries.

The stone cross now on display in the church is one of the finest Anglian examples of sculptured stone. It includes part of the poem *The Dream of the Rood*, written in runes.

Weston Park Museum, Western Bank, Sheffield S10 2TP. Tel. 01142 782600.

Exhibits include the Benty Grange helmet, excavated from an Anglo-Saxon grave by Thomas Bateman in 1848.

St Augustine's Abbey, Monastery Street, Canterbury, Kent CT1 1PF. Tel. 01227 378100.

Part of the Canterbury World Heritage Site, marking the site of the rebirth of Christianity in Southern England. St Augustine's was built to house the bodies of early Anglo-Saxon Christian kings.

Sutton Hoo, Woodbridge, Suffolk IP12 3DJ. Tel. 01394 389700.

Site of the famous seventh-century ship burial. Replicas of the treasures found in Mound 1 are on display at the Visitor Centre.

Taplow Burial, Taplow Court, Buckinghamshire SL6 0ER.

The burial mound lies within the grounds of the churchyard which grew up around it. The mound is accessible to visitors, but the grounds around it, belonging to Taplow Court Estate, can be visited by appointment.

West Stow Country Park and Anglo-Saxon Village, West Stow, Suffolk IP28 6HG. Tel. 01284 728718.

A stimulating reconstructed Anglo-Saxon village, closely based on the findings from the excavations at the site. The associated Visitor Centre Museum exhibits artefacts from major early Anglo-Saxon excavated sites in Suffolk.

City Museum, The Square, Winchester, Hampshire SO23 9ES. Tel. 01962 863064.

The Saxon floor of the museum houses some of the artefacts excavated in and around Anglo-Saxon Winchester, including the Winchester hanging bowl.

Whithorn Story Visitor Centre, Whithorn, Dumfries and Galloway, Scotland DG8 8NS. Tel. 01988 500508.

Visit the site of the Northumbrian monastery and view finds from the excavations on display at the visitor centre, as well as one of the best collections of early Christian carved stones in Britain.

Yeavering, Northumberland.

Arguably the most important Anglo-Saxon site in the country, the site of the Anglo-Saxon royal palace at Yeavering, excavated by Brian Hope-Taylor, is now owned by the Ad Gefrin Trust. The site, just north of the B6351, is open to the public, and information panels are available to explain its archaeology and history.

INDEX

Page numbers in italic refer to illustrations

Agriculture 13, 23, 24, 34–5

Alcoholic drinks 34, 37, 37

Animals: burial of 49–50, 54, 56, 65; as decoration 13, 50, 56–7, 56, 69; rearing/use of 21, 22, 23, 25, 28, 29, 30, 31, 34, 35, 36, 37, 49–50, 49, 57, 61, 62

Aristocracy 13, 23, 45, 54, 56, 61

Barrows (burial mounds) 51, 57

Bede, writings of 6, 8, 9, 11–12, 13, 24, 34, 35, 50, 57, 63, 67, 68, 69

Belts and buckles 41, 42, 43–4, 45, 57, 69

Board games 29, 54, 55

Boats/ships, use of 5, 29, 47–8, 50, 51, 55

Bones, use of 21, 28, 29, 31, 41, 54, 55, 69

Bowls 31, 37, 38

Buildings 7, 16, 69: features of 10, 18–19, 19, 20, 21, 24, 25; halls 10, 14, 16, 18, 19, 21, 22, 23–4, 23, 38, 53, 54, 56; houses 20, 22, 26, 39; huts 16, 17; materials used 10, 12, 14, 20, 22, 25, 26, 29, 32, 39; sunken-featured buildings 20–1, 22, 32, 69

Burial rituals 10–11, 67

Cemetery sites 9, 11, 16, 27, 33, 34, 35, 38, 38, 54, 55–6, 60, 65–6, 66, 66–7

Children: caring for 15–16, 17; education and training 59, 61,

63; naming of 17

Christianity, spread of 7, 11–13, 24–5, 39, 45, 50, 53, 54–5, 58, 63, 68–9, 69

Churches 12, 18, 25, 25, 26, 32, 55

Clothing 10, 11, 29, 41–4, 45: children's 45; men's 42, 43–4; women's 11, 11, 18, 40, 40, 42, 43, 44

Communal activities 17, 20–1, 23, 23, 37–8, 52, 53, 54

Cooking vessels/pots 11, 27, 28, 36–7, 37

Cremation sites/urns 9, 28, 38, 55–6, 57, 68

Cross shafts/crosses 13, 26, 53, 56, 58

Diet 21–2, 34, 35, 65–6

Divine protection 64, 69, 69

Doctors 68–9

Drinking vessels 37, 38, 38

Elite (the) 23, 43, 44, 44, 45, 49, 49, 50, 67

Family bonds/duties 15–16, 17, 17, 18, 63

Feasting 20, 23, 37, 38, 38, 53, 54, 67

Food/foodstuffs 11, 28, 28, 34, 35, 36–7, 36

Funerals 10, 37, 38, 39

Glass, use of 11, 31, 33, 38, 38, 41, 42

Graves/grave goods 10–11, 11, 32, 40, 66, 67, 69: animals 49–50, 54, 56, 65; boats/ships 5, 51, 54, 55; children's 16, 59, 69; costume 38, 41, 41, 42, 43–4, 68; men's 27, 30–1, 31, 33, 35, 37, 39, 42, 43–4, 43, 49–50, 53–4, 54, 55, 56, 57, 59, 62, 67; musical instruments 53–4, 62; weaponry 33, 35,

38, 43, 59, 60, 67; women's 12, 18, 30, 31, 31, 39, 41, 42, 59, 60, 61, 65, 68

Hair styles and tonsures 44, 45

Helmets 44, 45, 54, 56, 57

Illness and disease 16, 34, 63, 65–6, 66, 67, 68–9, 69

Industrial centres 28–9

Jewellery 10, 11, 11, 12, 16, 31, 32, 40, 41, 41, 42, 43, 44, 45, 45, 50, 56, 57, 57, 63, 67, 69

Keys 18, 19, 29, 41

Kings and kingdoms 11, 12, 12, 13, 18, 22, 23, 24–5, 26, 28, 45, 50, 51, 52, 53, 56, 57, 67

Law codes 15, 27, 50, 59, 61, 63

Leatherwork 30–1, 32, 41

Life expectancy 16, 65

Literacy 12, 12, 13, 53, 56, 57, 60, 63, 63

Marriage 11, 15–16, 18, 38, 61, 67

Medicine 13, 35, 36, 68–9, 69

Metalwork/smithing 11, 21, 29, 31, 32, 32, 33, 37, 38, 41, 42, 43, 45, 45, 51, 57, 57, 67

Music/musical instruments 52, 53–4, 62

Names/place names, meaning of 17–18, 36, 37, 55, 56

Pagan beliefs 50, 54, 55

Poetry/poems 13, 15, 53, 54, 56, 56, 57, 61–3

Pottery 21, 28–9, 28, 37, 41, 68

Pouches 11, 31, 40, 41, 43, 68

Ritual activity 50,

54–5, 57

River routes 39, 41, 46–7, 50–1, 50, 51

Roads 25–6, 49, 51

Sanitation 68

Servants/slaves 12, 13, 19, 25, 27, 35, 40, 49

Settlements, features of 9, 10, 10, 11, 20, 21, 21, 22, 23, 24, 26, 32, 35, 37, 38, 41, 49, 59, 68

Ship burials 5, 51, 55

Skeletons, evidence from 11, 16, 27, 27, 34, 65–6, 66, 66–7, 68

Starvation 27, 35–6, 65, 67

Storytelling 53

Sutton Hoo (Mound 1) 5, 35, 37, 37, 40, 43–4, 45, 49, 51, 53, 54, 55, 56, 57

Taxes 13, 26, 50

Textiles/weaving 21, 29–30, 29, 30, 31, 32, 41, 41, 42, 42, 43, 43, 44, 45, 59, 61, 62

Trade/trading sites 13, 26, 29, 35, 36, 37, 39–41, 39, 41, 46–7, 49, 50–1, 50

Travel/travellers 48, 49–51, 51

Tribal identities 7–10, 11

Warriors 44, 56

Water, importance of 13, 21, 36, 37, 69

Weaponry 11, 30, 31, 32, 33, 35, 43, 44, 50, 57, 57, 59, 60, 66, 67, 67

West Stow village 9, 10, 16, 18, 19, 20, 20, 22, 28, 29, 30, 31, 34–5, 38, 43, 61, 65, 68

Woodlands, importance of 13, 21, 22, 29, 34